SHIPS!

COME ABOARD

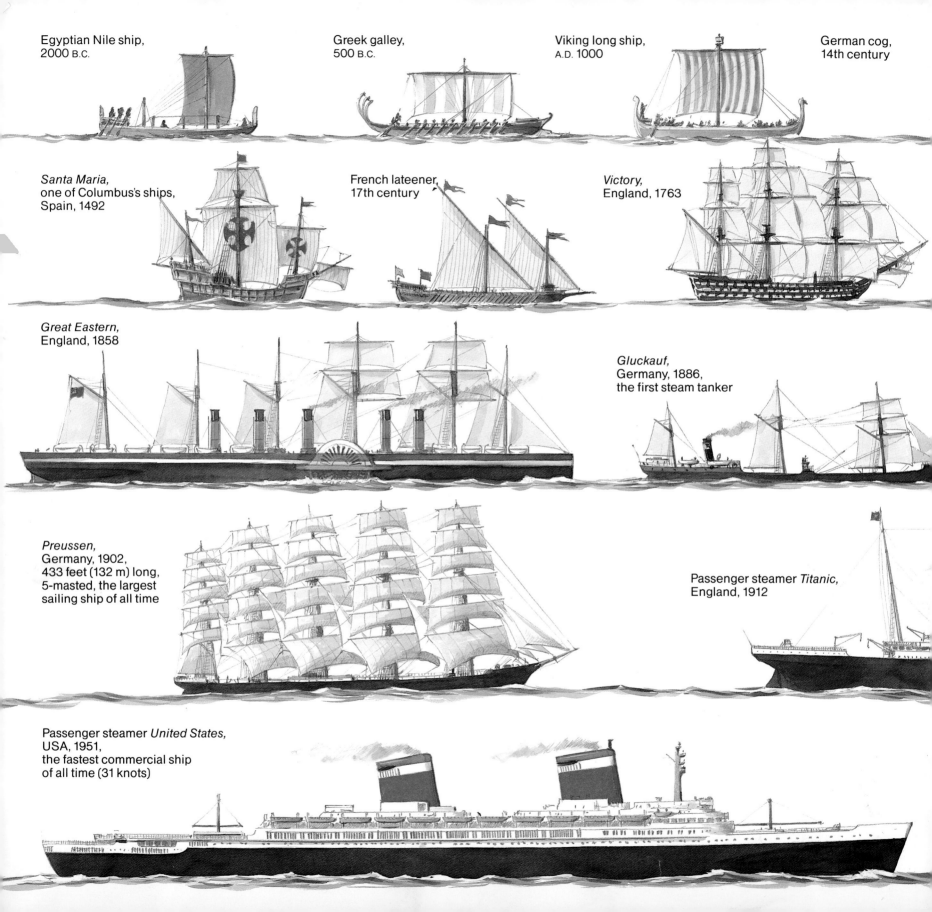

Egyptian Nile ship,
2000 B.C.

Greek galley,
500 B.C.

Viking long ship,
A.D. 1000

German cog,
14th century

Santa Maria,
one of Columbus's ships,
Spain, 1492

French lateener,
17th century

Victory,
England, 1763

Great Eastern,
England, 1858

Gluckauf,
Germany, 1886,
the first steam tanker

Preussen,
Germany, 1902,
433 feet (132 m) long,
5-masted, the largest
sailing ship of all time

Passenger steamer *Titanic,*
England, 1912

Passenger steamer *United States,*
USA, 1951,
the fastest commercial ship
of all time (31 knots)

Savannah,
USA, 1819

SHIPS!
COME ABOARD

Siegfried Aust ▪ illustrated by Enno Kleinert

Lerner Publications Company · Minneapolis

f Contents

. the Waterway 5

.ı Float to Kayak 6

Canoes 7

When the Wind Blows 8

War on the Sea 9

The Vikings Are Coming 10

Navigation 11

The Spanish Armada 12

Pirate Attack! 13

To Distant Shores 14

America Calls 15

Signposts at Sea 16

Under Full Sail 17

Full Steam Ahead 18

Anchors Aweigh! 19

Propellers 20

At Full Power 21

Cruise Ships 22

Fast, Faster, Fastest 23

Many Ships for Many Tasks 24

Cargo Ships 25

From Bow to Stern 26

Catastrophies at Sea 27

Search and Rescue 28

A Tour of the Harbor 29

Sea Travel around the World 30

ABC of Sea Travel 31

A Trip on the Waterway

Katy and John like to watch ships on the river. They learn about ships from their Uncle Hans, who is a barge captain. Today Hans has invited Katy and John on a trip along the river.

John tries to make out the names of the ships that come toward them. "Is that flat ship back there a freighter?" he asks Uncle Hans.

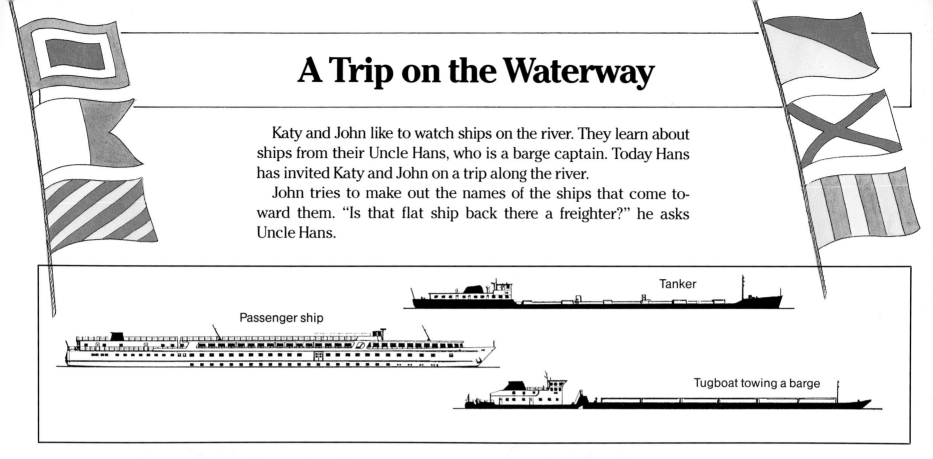

Tanker

Passenger ship

Tugboat towing a barge

"You can tell a lot about a craft by its shape," says Uncle Hans. "A flat ship like that is probably a tanker."

"There's so much to learn about ships!" Katy says.

A passenger ship sails alongside them, and the children wave to the people on deck.

5

Animal-skin float

From Float to Kayak

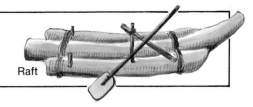
Raft

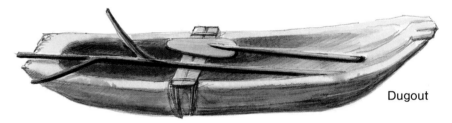
Egyptian papyrus boat

For many thousands of years, people have wanted to travel on the water—to hunt for food, to buy and sell goods, and to explore and conquer new lands.

The first boats were made of wood or blades of grass. People hollowed out tree trunks to make boats called *dugouts*. In ancient Egypt, people built boats of papyrus, the reedlike plant also used to make paper. The *hide boat* was made of an animal skin stretched across a wooden frame.

In places where wood and grass were scarce, people made boats entirely from animal skins. They sewed together and inflated the skins. An *animal-skin float* could be a one-person boat. Several floats tied together could support a *raft*. Rafts, flat bundles of tree branches or reeds, were useful for transporting people, livestock, or goods.

Hide boat

These early boats were moved and steered with a paddle. Some of them were very difficult to steer. Over the course of time, the shipbuilders' tools became better, and people learned more about how ships move on water. Skillful builders

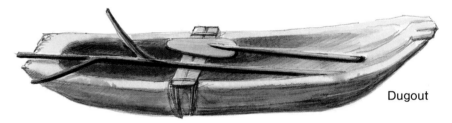
Dugout

designed boats that moved faster and were easier to steer.

The *kayak* is long and narrow, with an enclosed **deck.** The deck has one to four small openings where kayakers sit and power the boat with a double-sided paddle.

Kayaks are quick, agile, and light enough to be carried over ice. The kayak can go through rough water, because the enclosed deck keeps the boat from filling with water.

Kayaks are used mainly for recreation, although the Inuits (Eskimos) who built the first kayaks used the boats for hunting. The Inuits' kayaks were made of caribou hides or sealskins stretched over wooden frames.

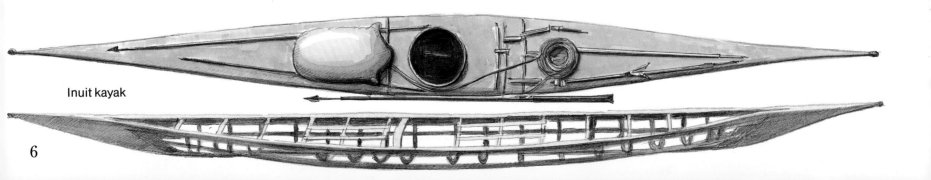
Inuit kayak

Canoes

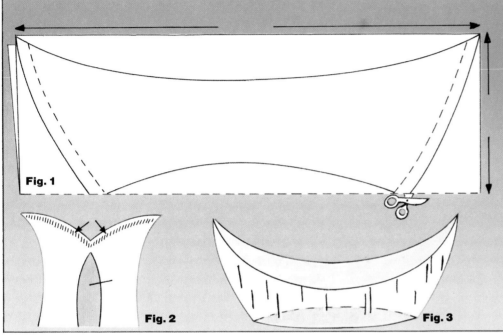

Fig. 1

Fig. 2

Fig. 3

Make a Canoe
Trace figure 1 at left on a piece of thin, transparent paper. Fold a piece of heavy construction paper in half. Lay the traced pattern on the fold line and cut the construction paper along the edges of the pattern. (Be careful not to cut through the fold at the front or the back!) Now overlap the shaded areas (figure 2) at each end of the canoe and glue them together. Your finished canoe will look like figure 3. To make your paper canoe waterproof, brush the outside lightly with vegetable oil.

In 1947 Thor Heyerdahl, a Norwegian explorer, sailed a balsawood raft called the *Kon-Tiki* on a famous voyage from Peru to the Polynesian islands in the Pacific Ocean. His voyage proved that South Americans could have traveled to the Polynesian islands long ago in the same type of crafts.

Canoes, which were invented by early North American Indians, are still counted among the world's finest boats. The Indians' canoes were crafted from bark—mainly birch bark—and fastened to a wooden frame. Canoes are moved and steered with a paddle. Large canoes are piloted by several paddlers.

The light, swift canoe was the perfect mode of transportation for traveling through North America's rivers and streams. Canada alone has as many waterways as the rest of the world put together. From almost anywhere in Canada's network of lakes and rivers, you can reach the shores of the great oceans.

During the 1600s, canoes were used to explore North America. The French explorers Louis Joliet and Father Jacques Marquette both traveled the Mississippi River by canoe.

Modern-day canoe with outer covering of rubberized fabric

Cedar canoe of the Huron Indians of Canada

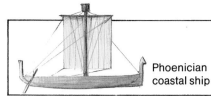
When the Wind Blows

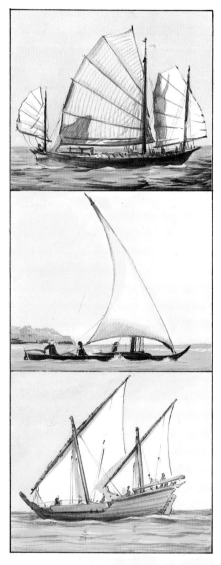

Top: Chinese and Japanese junks have sails that look like window blinds—made of horizontal strips of cloth.

Middle: African outrigger canoes, with a single sail, traveled the coasts and were used for fishing.

Bottom: Arabian trading ships, called dhows, have triangular sails called lateens.

Egyptians learned to build long, narrow boats called *galleys* in about 4000 B.C. The first galleys were made of reeds and powered by a row of paddlers.

Egyptians then learned to use the wind to power their boats. They began using sails about 3200 B.C. Large rectangular sails made from woven papyrus, and later from woven cloth, were set to the wind. If the wind stopped blowing, the pole holding the sail, called a **mast**, was laid down and rowers took over.

In about 3000 B.C., Egyptians learned to build boats from planks of wood. The wooden ships' bodies, or **hulls,** were painted green like papyrus. The sailors believed that they could keep away crocodiles and evil spirits with the green paint. Three **rudders,** flat pieces of wood attached to the ship's **stern,** steered the ship. Paddlers on each side drove the boat forward.

These early Egyptian ships were used chiefly on the Nile River. They were rather light ships that wouldn't have been sturdy enough to go on the rough waters of the sea.

The Minoans, people who lived on the island of Crete, were the first sailors on the Mediterranean Sea. Their ships resembled the Egyptian ships, with large, rectangular sails, called square sails, and rudders. But the Minoan ships were stronger than the Egyptian ships since they could withstand the storms at sea.

Later, after about 1200 B.C., Greeks and Phoenicians, the people of the ancient country called Phoenicia, built ships for the Mediterranean, too. In about 500 B.C., they built the first ships with two masts. The second mast and sail made steering easier.

Egyptian merchant ship, about 2000 B.C.

War on the Sea

Greek warship   Roman galley

In ancient times, a warship was an important weapon. The front part of the ship, called the **bow,** was used to hit an enemy galley, tear apart its hull, and sink it. Warships needed great speed for ramming, much more than the wind on the ship's small sails would provide. Before battle, the sails were taken down and rowers took over.

At first, longer and longer ships were built in order to increase the number of seats for rowers. But longer ships proved to be unwieldy in battle and broke apart on rough seas.

Biremes, invented by the Greeks in about 700 B.C., had a second row of oars above the first. The galley doubled its power without doubling its length. *Triremes,* invented in about 650 B.C., seated three levels of rowers. For speed, triremes were superior to any opponent. About 170 rowers and some 30 officers and soldiers made up the crew.

Rowers in a three-rowed trireme (left) and in a two-rowed bireme (right)

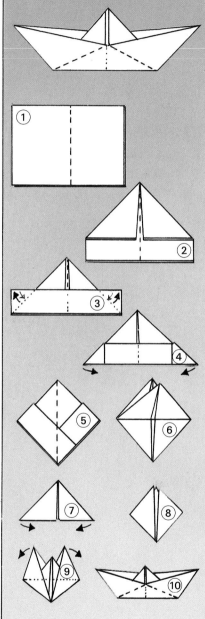

Follow the diagram, from steps 1 to 10, to make a simple paper boat. Or stop after step 4 and you will have an admiral's hat.

The Vikings Are Coming

The early inhabitants of Scandinavia, called Vikings, were people of the sea. The sea almost surrounded their homeland, and fjords (inlets of the sea) cut into the Scandinavian coastline. Water travel was the main form of transportation in the region. Because of overcrowding and a shortage of farmland, Vikings became traders, conquerors, and explorers. Their thirst for conquest took them all over Europe, and even to Greenland and North America. They needed strong ships for such long journeys.

Vikings built two main kinds of ships, both of wood. Their roomy trading ships, called *knorrs*, measured about 50 feet (15 meters) long. Viking warships, called *long ships,* ranged in length from 65 to 95 feet (20 to 29 m).

At sea, a Viking ship depended mainly on wind and the ship's large woolen sail. On rivers and in battle, rowers powered the ships. Most Viking long ships had 20 oars on each side, and some larger ships had 30.

The *cog,* invented in about A.D. 1200, became a standard warship in northern Europe. Cogs had a large rudder in the middle of the stern and a high deck called a *castle* at the stern and prow.

The Vikings attached a **keel,** a long, narrow piece of wood, to the underside of their ships. The keel kept the ship steady and made it faster and easier to steer.

The **prow** (front end) of Viking warships curved upward and ended with a woodcarving of an animal head, usually of a dragon or snake.

Navigation

In 1805 British Rear Admiral Sir Thomas Beaufort developed a table describing the stages of winds—from calm to hurricane force—and their effect on water. The Beaufort Scale is used all over the world.

0 No wind; smooth sea

1 Light air; ripples in water

2 Light breeze; small waves

3 Gentle breeze; small waves, some whitecaps

4 Moderate breeze; small waves, many whitecaps

5 "Fresh" (brisk) breeze; moderate waves, many whitecaps, spray

6 Strong breeze; large waves, foamy crests, spray

7 Moderate gale; high seas, breaking crests, spray

8 Fresh gale; high and long waves, spray

9 Strong gale; high waves, wide streaks of foam, spray

10 Whole gale; very high waves, sea all white

11 Storm; extremely high waves, low visibility (the distance you see)

12 Hurricane; driving spray, low visibility

Centuries ago, sailors had to rely entirely on sight to guide their ships. A sailor called a lookout would watch over the water from high up on a ship's mast. The lookout watched for landmarks such as islands, mountains, and buildings on shore.

Ancient navigators also observed the stars and planets. With an instrument called a **sextant,** they measured the angle between a planet or star and the horizon. When they applied this measurement to a mathematical equation, they could determine the position of the ship.

Navigators still use these ancient methods of navigation, along with newer methods. They now use charts that show the features of a waterway, such as the depth of the water and the location of islands. They use a **compass,** a device for determining directions. And since the development of radio, navigators have used electronic navigation systems that use radio signals.

Radar (*ra*dio *d*etecting *a*nd *r*anging) is a very popular electronic navigation method that uses radio waves. Special devices send radio waves toward an object and pick up the waves when they bounce back. How quickly the waves return, and from which direction they return, determines the object's location. Radar is used to prevent collisions with other ships and to avoid dangerous objects in the water.

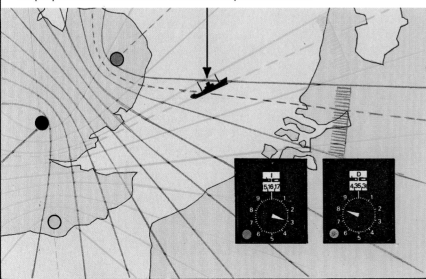

Loran (long-range navigation): Radio signals (represented by solid red and green lines, below) are sent from three different stations—a master station (shown here as a black dot) and two slave stations (red and green dots). Receivers on a ship pick up the signals. A navigator reads the signals and plots lines of position (dotted lines) on a chart. The ship's position is where the two lines of position cross.

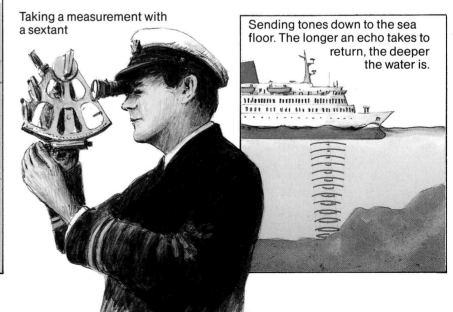

Taking a measurement with a sextant

Sending tones down to the sea floor. The longer an echo takes to return, the deeper the water is.

The Spanish Armada

18th-century stern lamp

16th-century cannon

In the mid-1580s, King Philip II of Spain began to assemble a fleet of warships, or *armada*. For years English ships had raided the Spanish silver fleet. It was time for Spain to take control of the seas.

In 1588, with more than 150 ships and a crew of 30,000, the Spanish Armada threatened England. English ships were awaiting the Spanish offshore, and they shot their cannons from a short distance. When their gunpowder ran out, they shot burning arrows from long bows at the Spanish and set their sails on fire.

After a nine-day battle, the Armada fled across the North Sea. There, heavy storms

Many people called the Spanish Armada the "Invincible Armada," because they thought the fleet couldn't be defeated.

wrecked many of the ships. Ten thousand men were lost at sea, and the mighty Armada was defeated.

In this famous sea battle, both the Spanish and English fleets used ships called *galleons*. Galleons were big ships with high sterncastles. They were sometimes hard to steer because they carried so many heavy guns.

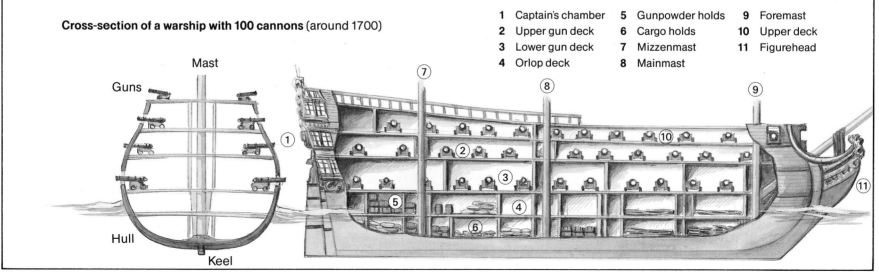

Cross-section of a warship with 100 cannons (around 1700)

1 Captain's chamber	5 Gunpowder holds	9 Foremast
2 Upper gun deck	6 Cargo holds	10 Upper deck
3 Lower gun deck	7 Mizzenmast	11 Figurehead
4 Orlop deck	8 Mainmast	

Mast

Guns

Hull

Keel

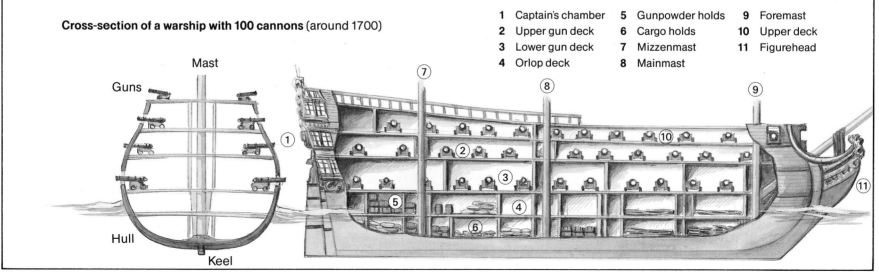

Pirate Attack!

A foreign craft has approached the Spanish ship in the course of the night. Now, in the gray morning light, the Spanish sailors see the pirate flag. Fear overcomes them—fear for their cargo of silver and for their own lives.

As the sailors distribute muskets, sabers, and knives among themselves, the pirates fire their guns. Wood splinters, cries fill the air....

Ship robbers, called pirates, have existed for thousands of years in all parts of the world. But the most looting done by pirates occurred from the 16th through the 18th centuries, on the Mediterranean and Caribbean seas.

Besides valuable cargo, or goods, the pirates often captured top-secret sea charts and records. If they learned certain ships' routes, the pirates could lie in wait for the ships.

In the past, keeping time on a ship was difficult. The rocking motion of a ship affected clocks with pendulums, so the clocks would not keep accurate time. Early sailors had to keep time with an hourglass.

You can build an hourglass yourself!

Fill a bottle half full with fine, dry sand. Glue a piece of cardboard over the bottle's opening.

Poke a hole in the middle of the cardboard with a knitting needle or a large nail.

Glue a second bottle upside-down, on top of the first bottle. Glue a strip of wood to both sides of the bottles to give your hourglass support.

Hints: Be sure to use a glue that bonds wood, cardboard, and glass. You can secure the wood strips with rubber bands or string while the glue is drying.

To Distant Shores

and his ships, the *Nina,* the *Pinta,* and the *Santa Maria*

In about the mid-1400s, Mediterranean shipbuilders combined the best features of existing ships to build a new ship called a *square rigger.* The square rigger became the standard ship throughout Europe for about 300 years.

Steering oars were replaced with a large rudder at the stern, and the sails were enlarged to give the ship more power. The basic square rigger had three masts: a **mainmast** in the middle and a **foremast** in the front, each which held a big square sail and a smaller square sail up above. A **mizzenmast** in back held a triangular **lateen** sail, and a pole stuck out from the bow carried a small square sail. Explorers of the 1400s and 1500s such as Christopher Columbus used ships rigged this way.

The English explorer James Cook was also a great sailor. Cook sailed the *Endeavour* to New Zealand and Australia in 1769 and 1770. He commanded two other voyages to the Pacific, and he sailed around the world twice.

The *Endeavour*

America Calls

The early English settlers of New England, called Pilgrims, arrived on the *Mayflower* in 1620. A steady stream of immigration to the American colonies soon began. Thousands of Europeans were attracted to North America's vast, unsettled land. But the journey was long and the cost was high.

Poor people traveled cheaply by cooking their own meals and sleeping on straw or on blankets they brought with them. People could not depend on the ships to sail at regular times. A ship would not set out on the voyage across the Atlantic until it was completely full.

By the early 1800s, the increase in immigration to the United States created a great demand for better passenger service. Beginning in 1818, a new service was offered— ships that sailed on regular schedules. *Packet ships* set sail whether or not they were full.

The *Mayflower*

Passengers on an emigrant ship   (based on an antique engraving)

A fully-rigged ship: In addition to sails and masts, a ship's rigging consists of *booms* and *gaffs,* the poles that hold the masts straight out. Ropes, called *lines,* are also part of the rigging. *Shrouds* are lines that run from the sides of the boat to the masts. *Stays* run from the bow and stern to the masts.

Signposts at Sea

Buoy

Columbus saw the coast too late and ran aground with the *Santa Maria*. The accident happened near present-day Haiti on Christmas Eve, 1492.

The water holds many hidden dangers, especially in fog and in storms. Just as traffic signs guide cars and buses, there are signs on the water that show ships the way.

Buoys, steel markers anchored to the sea floor, warn sailors of underwater dangers such as wrecks and sandbars. Buoys are also used to mark narrow waterways known as channels. Buoys are painted with different colors and numbers, which tell sailors how to pass the buoy—on the right or on the left. Some buoys have lights so that sailors can see them at night. Some are equipped with whistles, bells, or horns. Even when a lighted buoy can't be seen through thick fog, a ship's pilot can hear a buoy's horn or bell.

A **lighthouse** is a tower that has a very bright light on top. Lighthouses have been used for centuries. Many years ago, their lights were wood- or oil-burning fires. Now they have electric lights. A lighthouse's signal light may be colored, and each lighthouse has its own pattern of flashing light. Lighthouses are built in slightly different shapes and painted different colors. If sailors can see and identify a particular lighthouse, they will know where their ship is on the water.

A lighthouse beam flashes in rapid bursts (1). The lighthouse keeper works in the service room (2). Below that are the kitchen (3), bedroom (4), and storage cellar (5). Drinking water is collected in a tank called a cistern (6). The keeper can know how high the water is outside by looking at the water gauge (7).

Wooden pulley used for setting sail

Under Full Sail

Cape Horn

At wind speed 5 on the Beaufort Scale, a ship runs under full sail. The stronger the wind, the less sail surface is needed.

Wind speed 6 or 7

Wind speed 8 or 9

Slender, streamlined *clippers*, first built in the 1840s, were the fastest ships of their time. In fact, their name comes from the word "clip," which means to move swiftly. Clippers had as many as 6 sails to a mast, and some clippers had as many as 35 sails. Under full sail, a clipper could travel at 18 to 20 **knots,** or nautical miles per hour.

The United States built the first clippers. Called Yankee Clippers, these ships were designed to sail from the East Coast to China—to bring back tea and other goods. At the time, ships sailing to China had to sail around the tip of South America. There, the fierce storms of Cape Horn slowed many voyages. Some ships made the trip in 200 days, while the fastest clippers needed fewer than 90 days.

Each sail has a name:

1	flying jib	12	main topsail
2	outer jib	13	main topgallant
3	inner jib	14	main royal
4	foresail	15	mizzen-topmast staysail
5	fore topsail	16	mizzen-topgallant staysail
6	Shanti Shah	17	mizzen topsail
7	foreroyal	18	mizzen topgallant
8	main-topmast staysail	19	mizzen-royal sail
9	main-topgallant staysail	20	mizzen skysail
10	main-royal staysail	21	spanker
11	mainsail		

Full Steam Ahead

In strong winds, clippers were unbeatable for speed. But shipbuilders still hoped to design a ship that could move without windpower. As early as the 1700s, inventors had begun experimenting with steam engines to power boats.

Steam engines have two main parts—a furnace and a boiler. In the furnace, fuel is burned to produce heat energy. In the boiler, the heat energy changes water into steam. The production of steam creates energy that can be used to power a machine.

The first steam sailing ships burned coal in their furnaces. The steam power turned paddlewheels on both sides of the boat. Later boats were built with paddles at the stern.

The *Clermont,* designed and built by American Robert Fulton, was the first commercially successful steamboat. The boat provided regular passenger service on the Hudson River in New York beginning in 1807. People liked the dependable steamship, which was able to set sail even in dead calm. By the early 1900s, the steamship had nearly replaced ships with sails.

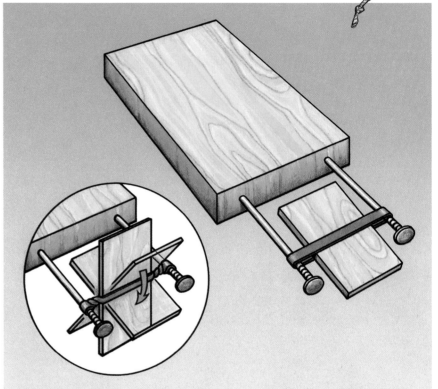

With just a few inexpensive materials, you can make a paddlewheel boat. You'll need a small block of wood (the end of a 2 x 4, if available), two long nails, a fat rubber band, and a small, thin wood scrap to use as a paddle. Hammer the nails into one end of the wood block, as far apart as possible. Just pound them enough so they won't pull out. Stretch the rubber band over the ends of the nails. Wind up your paddle in the rubber band, and you're ready for your first launch!

In 1870 the *Robert E. Lee* raced on the Mississippi River from New Orleans to St. Louis. The boat reached the finish line 3 hours and 44 minutes before its competitor, the *Natchez.*

Anchors Aweigh!

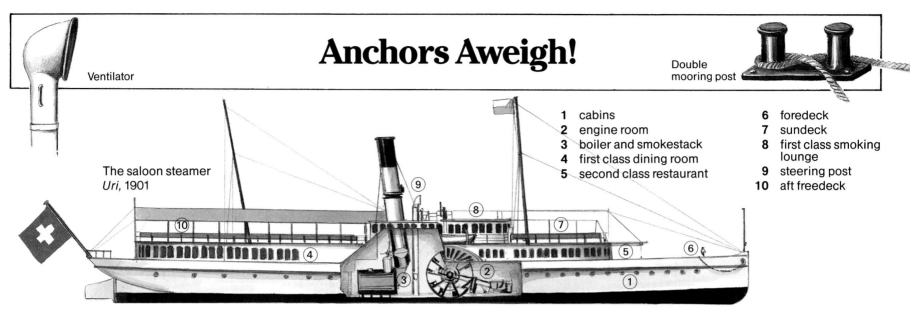

Ventilator

Double mooring post

The saloon steamer *Uri*, 1901

1 cabins
2 engine room
3 boiler and smokestack
4 first class dining room
5 second class restaurant
6 foredeck
7 sundeck
8 first class smoking lounge
9 steering post
10 aft freedeck

At first the large steam engines and boilers were installed on existing sailing ships. Soon new steamships were built that were bigger and more comfortable for travelers.

The *Great Eastern,* with a length of 692 feet (211m) and a width of 85 feet (26m), was a gigantic ship. But when the ship was first launched, it glided only a few yards. On another trial run, the boiler exploded. Because of its shaky start, not enough passengers could be attracted to it. The *Great Eastern* was eventually converted into a cablelayer. In the 1860s, it was used to lay the first underwater transatlantic telephone cable.

About the same time that steam power was being developed, British shipbuilders were beginning to make ships of iron. Iron ships were stronger, safer, and easier to repair than wooden ships. During the late 1880s, steel began to replace iron for ships. Steel ships were stronger and lighter than iron ships.

The *Great Eastern*

Anchor

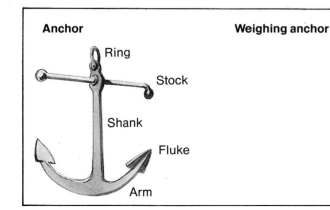

Ring
Stock
Shank
Fluke
Arm

Weighing anchor

Anchor glides over sea bed

Anchor catches

Anchor holds on

Propellers

While paddlewheel boats were good for rivers, they were not very good on rough seas. Paddlewheels were often damaged by driftwood or high waves. And when a ship rocked from side to side, one wheel and then the other could lift completely out of the water, wasting power. The problem was solved with the invention of the ship's screw, or **propeller**, which attached to a ship's stern. A propeller remained wholly underwater and could move a ship much faster than a paddlewheel could.

People still use propeller-driven boats for very fast travel over short distances. A *hydrofoil* is a boat mounted on foils (wings that skim near the surface of the water). The hull of the boat rises up out of the water, and the boat can reach speeds of up to 80 knots.

An air-cushion vehicle, also called a *hovercraft,* uses a powerful fan to produce a continuous thrust of air between the boat and the water. Propellers drive the boat forward, and the hovercraft rides the cushion of air to speeds of up to 70 knots.

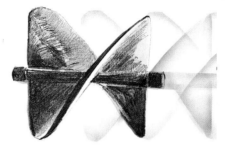

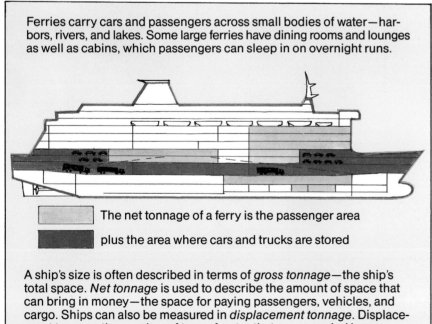

Ferries carry cars and passengers across small bodies of water—harbors, rivers, and lakes. Some large ferries have dining rooms and lounges as well as cabins, which passengers can sleep in on overnight runs.

The net tonnage of a ferry is the passenger area

plus the area where cars and trucks are stored

A ship's size is often described in terms of *gross tonnage*—the ship's total space. *Net tonnage* is used to describe the amount of space that can bring in money—the space for paying passengers, vehicles, and cargo. Ships can also be measured in *displacement tonnage*. Displacement tons are the number of tons of water that are occupied by, or displaced by, a ship.

A hydrofoil on a voyage

At Full Power!

As people built faster and faster ships, they also improved engine design. Steam engines were very powerful, but their great weight slowed down the ships. A better ship engine was designed by a German engineer named Rudolf Diesel. Not only was the new engine smaller and lighter than a steam engine, but it also used oil as fuel, which was cheaper than coal. The small but enormously powerful *diesel engine* rapidly replaced the steam engine in ships.

In the 1950s and 1960s, the United States, Japan, and West Germany all built ships run by nuclear power, the energy created when atoms of uranium, a silvery-white metal, are split. Nuclear powered ships have not become popular, however, because of the high cost of building and running them.

Gasoline engines burn a mixture of gasoline vapor and air inside a cylinder that contains a piston. When the gas-air mixture burns, different hot gases form. The gases expand and push on the pistons, causing them to move. The movement can turn a wheel or a propeller.

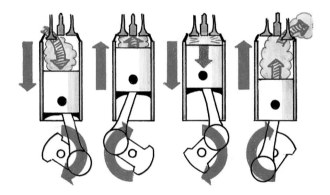

Gasoline engines are often used to power speedboats. This gasoline engine has four cylinders.

Aircraft carriers became very important in World War II. Airplanes were stored on the carrier, and planes took off from the large flight deck that reached from bow to stern.

Cruise Ships

The early 1900s were the age of the ocean liner. Competition between shipping lines created larger and more luxurious ships. The *Normandie* of France and the *Queen Mary* and *Queen Elizabeth* of England were three of the most elegant ships ever built. These "floating hotels" of the 1930s had gourmet restaurants, ballrooms, and luxury suites on board.

The airplane has ended the reign of the ocean liner, but many people still travel on cruise ships that sail the Mediterranean Sea, the Caribbean Sea, and other popular vacation areas. On cruise ships, people still enjoy fine meals, dancing, and live entertainment. Cruise ships also make frequent stops so that passengers can visit towns and fishing spots along the water.

Fast, Faster, Fastest

The Blue Riband trophy

Important title holders of the Blue Riband:

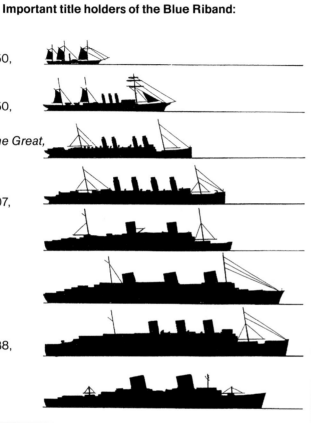

Asia,
Great Britain, 1850,
12.1 knots

City of Paris,
Great Britain, 1850,
19.5 knots

Kaiser Wilhelm the Great,
Germany, 1897,
22.3 knots

Mauretania,
Great Britain, 1907,
23.7 knots

Bremen,
Germany, 1929,
27.9 knots

Normandie,
France, 1935,
30.5 knots

Queen Mary,
Great Britain, 1938,
30.7 knots

United States,
USA, 1952,
35.9 knots

As the great quest for speed continued, ships competed against each other in exciting races. An award called the Blue Riband was given to the ship making the fastest crossing of the Atlantic, from Bishop Rock, England, to New York. During the 1930s, the ocean liners *Normandie* and *Queen Mary* competed for the Blue Riband.

When World War II broke out, the *Normandie* remained in New York. The U.S. Navy took the ship over and used it under the name *Lafayette*. Then, in 1942, a fire broke out on the ship's upper deck. As the New York Fire Department pumped tons of water into the ship's body, the ship became topheavy and capsized at the pier. The *Lafayette* was righted, but it was not repaired again. The once-great ship was finally scrapped.

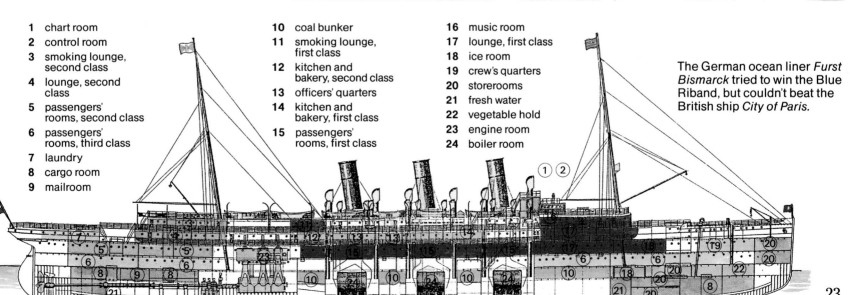

1	chart room
2	control room
3	smoking lounge, second class
4	lounge, second class
5	passengers' rooms, second class
6	passengers' rooms, third class
7	laundry
8	cargo room
9	mailroom
10	coal bunker
11	smoking lounge, first class
12	kitchen and bakery, second class
13	officers' quarters
14	kitchen and bakery, first class
15	passengers' rooms, first class
16	music room
17	lounge, first class
18	ice room
19	crew's quarters
20	storerooms
21	fresh water
22	vegetable hold
23	engine room
24	boiler room

The German ocean liner *Furst Bismarck* tried to win the Blue Riband, but couldn't beat the British ship *City of Paris.*

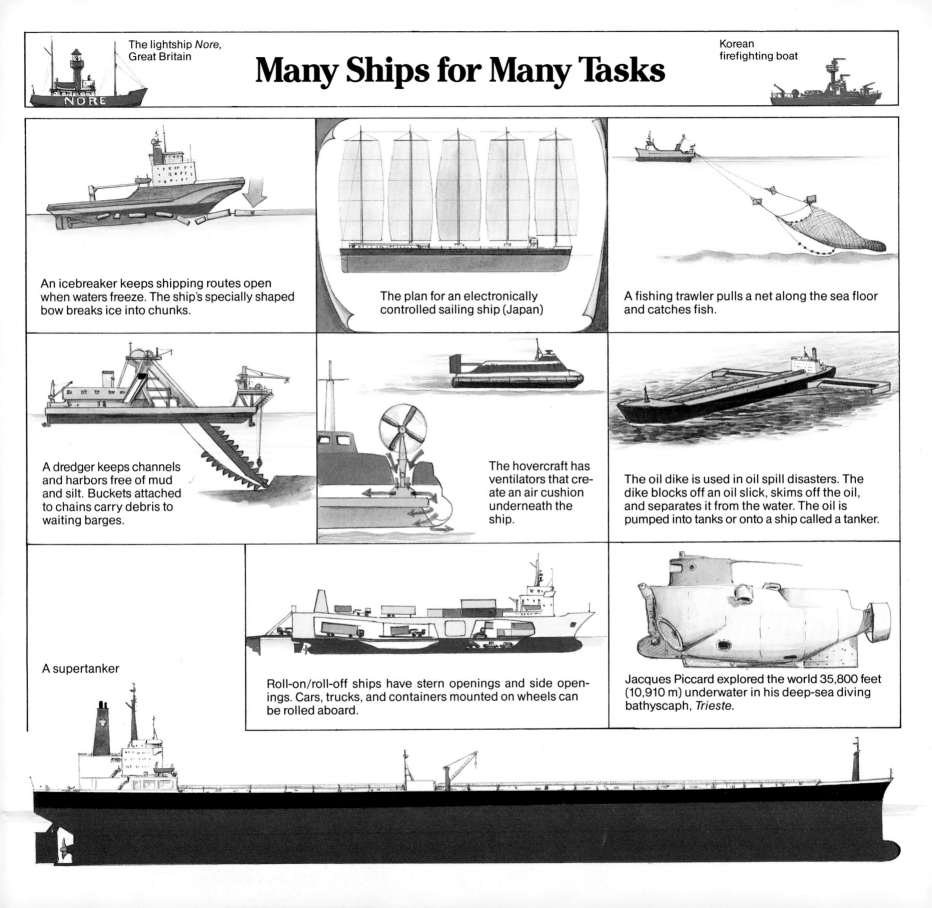

Many Ships for Many Tasks

The lightship *Nore*, Great Britain

Korean firefighting boat

An icebreaker keeps shipping routes open when waters freeze. The ship's specially shaped bow breaks ice into chunks.

The plan for an electronically controlled sailing ship (Japan)

A fishing trawler pulls a net along the sea floor and catches fish.

A dredger keeps channels and harbors free of mud and silt. Buckets attached to chains carry debris to waiting barges.

The hovercraft has ventilators that create an air cushion underneath the ship.

The oil dike is used in oil spill disasters. The dike blocks off an oil slick, skims off the oil, and separates it from the water. The oil is pumped into tanks or onto a ship called a tanker.

A supertanker

Roll-on/roll-off ships have stern openings and side openings. Cars, trucks, and containers mounted on wheels can be rolled aboard.

Jacques Piccard explored the world 35,800 feet (10,910 m) underwater in his deep-sea diving bathyscaph, *Trieste*.

Cargo Ships

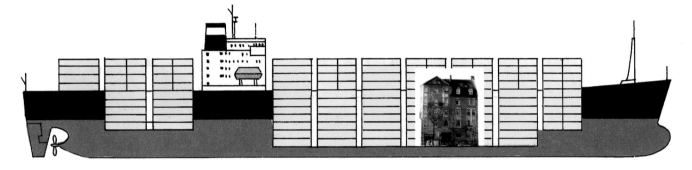

This fully loaded cargo ship is taller than a five-story building!

While the use of passenger ships has declined, many ships are still used for transporting cargo. A large cargo ship, also called a *freighter,* can carry more than 500,000 tons of oil, for example—much more than an airplane could hold.

Tankers, the ships that carry liquids such as oil and gasoline, are some of the biggest cargo ships. A very large tanker is called a *supertanker.* These ships, with lengths of more than 1,500 feet (457 m), need several miles to turn or stop. And because they are so long, they are difficult to navigate. Tanker accidents may cause oil spills that create tremendous damage to the environment. To help prevent accidents, tankers are computer controlled.

Dry bulk carriers are ships that transport grain, coal, and other solid cargoes that can be loaded in bulk—in one large area of the ship without containers. *General cargo ships* carry products such as cars, machines, and food. *Multipurpose cargo ships* may carry a combination of different kinds of cargo.

Unloading cargo with cranes

From Bow to Stern

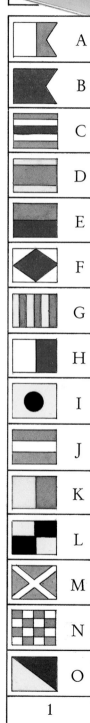

A	
B	
C	
D	
E	
F	
G	
H	
I	
J	
K	
L	
M	
N	
O	

Do you know why a ship floats? When you climb into a bathtub, watch the surface of the water rise around you. Your body has displaced, or moved, the water. Then put just your arm underwater. Can you feel how the water pushes it up? Water's ability to hold an object up is called **buoyancy.** But water will not hold an object that is heavier than the water itself. A heavy ship floats because water is heavy, too. A ship is lighter than the water it displaces.

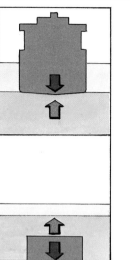

International Flag Code

The International Flag Code is a system of communication that uses flags. To send messages with flags, sailors raise one to five groups of flags that have code meanings or spell out words. Repeater flags are used to substitute for a flag that has already been used in a message. Repeater flags make it unnecessary for sailors to carry extra sets of flags.

On this mixed-cargo freighter, the *ram bow* (1), a specially shaped bow, gives the ship more speed. Cranes called *derricks* (2) on the *masts* (3) bring cargo through openings called *cargo hatches* (4) on deck. *Load lines* (5) show how full the ship may be loaded safely. Fresh water is lighter than salt water, and warm tropical water is not as buoyant as cold water. *Depth marks* (6) show how deep the ship's keel sits in the water. From the raised deck called the *bridge* (7), the *rudder* (8) and the *propeller* (9) are controlled. The *radar antenna* (10) picks up radio signals. In case of accidents, *lifeboats* (11) are on board. *Ventilators* (12) on

the *foredeck* (13) let in fresh air. A device called a *capstan* (14) moves the *anchor* (15). On a rough sea, *railings* (16) keep sailors from going overboard. The *national flag* (17) on the *poop* (18), or rear deck, shows the ship's country of origin. The *symbol* (19) on the *funnel* (20) and the *shipping company's flag* (21) identify the ship's owner.

P	
Q	
R	
S	
T	
U	
V	
W	
X	
Y	
Z	
	Reply flag
	First repeater flag
	Second repeater flag
	Third repeater flag

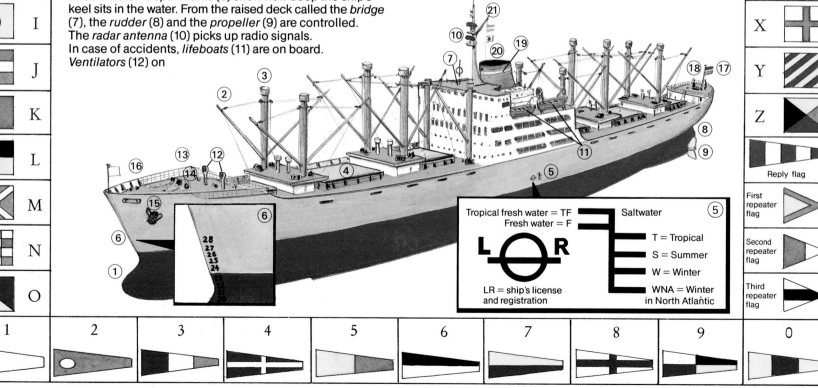

Tropical fresh water = TF
Fresh water = F
Saltwater

T = Tropical
S = Summer
W = Winter
WNA = Winter in North Atlantic

LR = ship's license and registration

1	2	3	4	5	6	7	8	9	0

The *Titanic*, a British steamer, was the largest, most modern passenger ship of its day. It was said to be unsinkable. But during the night of April 14-15, 1912, on its very first voyage, the mighty *Titanic* collided with an iceberg. The collision opened a gash almost 300 feet (91 m) wide across the ship's **starboard** (right) side. There weren't enough lifeboats to hold all the people aboard. When the ship sank, it took 1,500 passengers into the icy waters of the Atlantic. Just 705 people survived.

Morse Code Alphabet

Morse code is a system of dots, dashes, and spaces that was once used to send messages by telegraph.

A •—	J •———	S •••	1 •————
B —•••	K —•—	T —	2 ••———
C —•—•	L •—••	U ••—	3 •••——
D —••	M ——	V •••—	4 ••••—
E •	N —•	W •——	5 •••••
F ••—•	O ———	X —••—	6 —••••
G ——•	P •——•	Y —•——	7 ——•••
H ••••	Q ——•—	Z ——••	8 ———••
I ••	R •—•		9 ————•
			0 —————

International Distress Signals: All these signals mean "Send help!"

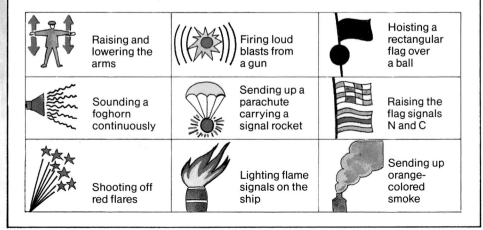

Raising and lowering the arms	Firing loud blasts from a gun	Hoisting a rectangular flag over a ball
Sounding a foghorn continuously	Sending up a parachute carrying a signal rocket	Raising the flag signals N and C
Shooting off red flares	Lighting flame signals on the ship	Sending up orange-colored smoke

The heavy winds and rain of hurricanes have caused many fatal shipwrecks.

MAYDAY

Search and Rescue

In 1789, the British ship *Adventure* sank less than 1,000 feet (300m) from shore as a crowd of people watched helplessly. Soon after this, the lifeboat was invented.

Lifeboats are vessels used to rescue people in danger. They are strong boats, designed to withstand the roughest waves. Some lifeboats are even self-righting. If they capsize, they will automatically right themselves. Ships also carry life vests, lifeboats, or inflatable liferafts.

Some ships also carry distress buoys. If the ship sinks, the buoys send automatic distress calls with information about the ship's position. The buoys send radio signals to a satellite, which alerts people at a tracking station of the accident.

Rescue service
Shore watch
Coastal authority — Telephone connections
Medical care
Ocean survey
Weather service

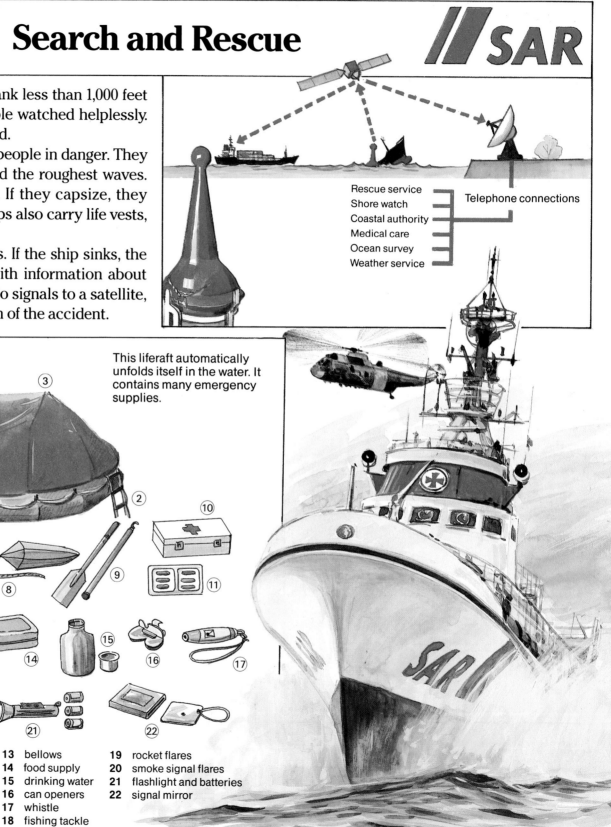

This liferaft automatically unfolds itself in the water. It contains many emergency supplies.

1	compressed air supply	7	sponge	13 bellows
2	boarding ladder	8	anchor	14 food supply
3	locator light	9	paddle	15 drinking water
4	rescue floats	10	first-aid kit	16 can openers
5	knife	11	seasickness medicine	17 whistle
6	bucket	12	tools	18 fishing tackle

19 rocket flares
20 smoke signal flares
21 flashlight and batteries
22 signal mirror

A Tour of the Harbor

Harbor ferry

Harbor tugboat

"Toooot." The ferry takes off (1) and the tour of the harbor begins. On the **port** (left) side, a dockyard (2) appears. The tour ship sails into a bend in the harbor where the announcer points out a berth (3), the area where ships lay anchor.

The tour goes past a quay, or loading area (4), a berth for mixed-cargo freighters (5), and the rebuilding of a ship at a shipyard (6). In another part of the harbor, coal is being unloaded (7). Cold goods are stored in giant cold storage bins (8) while fruit ripens in a special station (9). The floating dock (10) can be towed wherever it is needed.

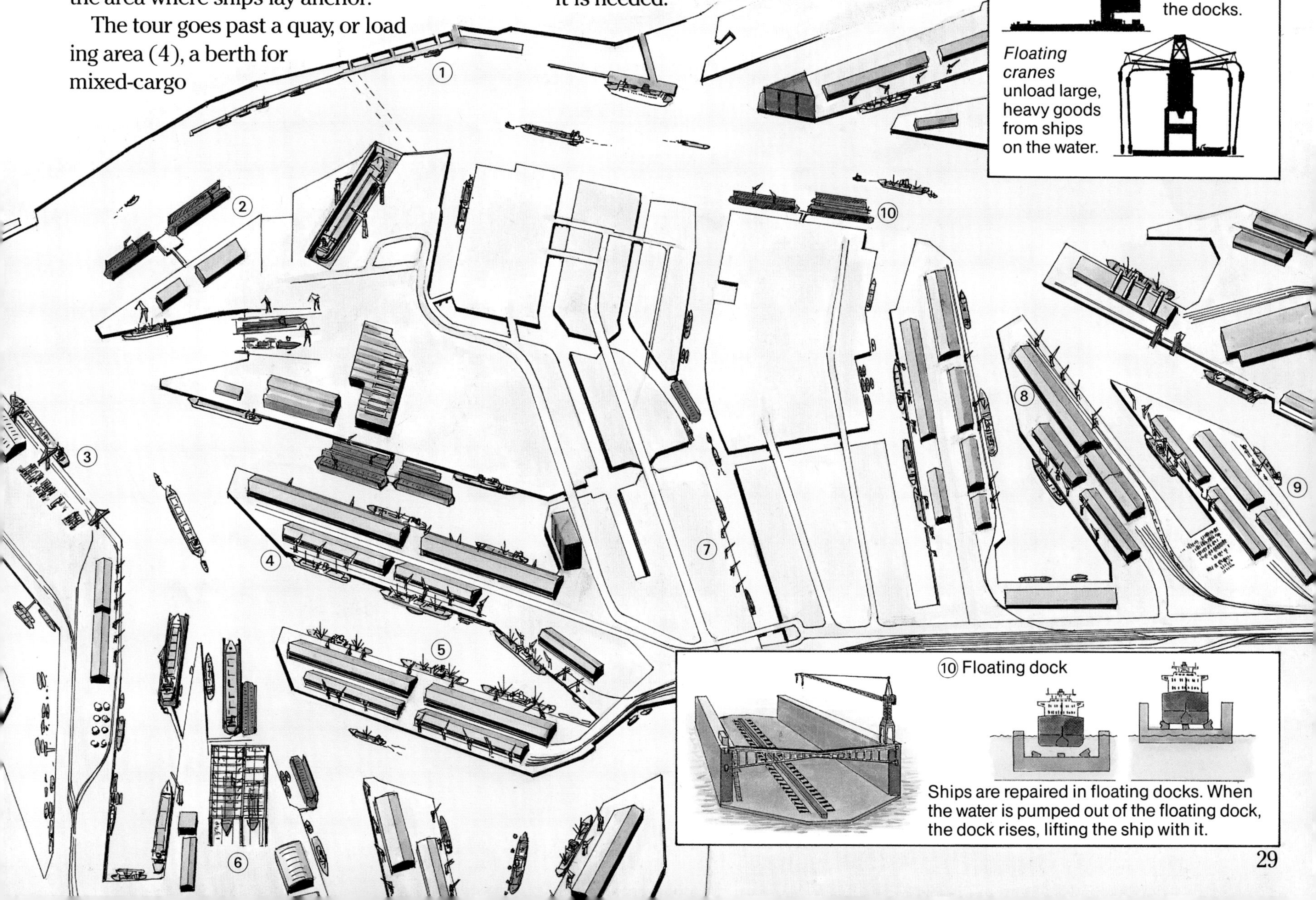

A *grain siphon* sucks loose grain from a cargo ship into containers on the docks.

Floating cranes unload large, heavy goods from ships on the water.

⑩ Floating dock

Ships are repaired in floating docks. When the water is pumped out of the floating dock, the dock rises, lifting the ship with it.

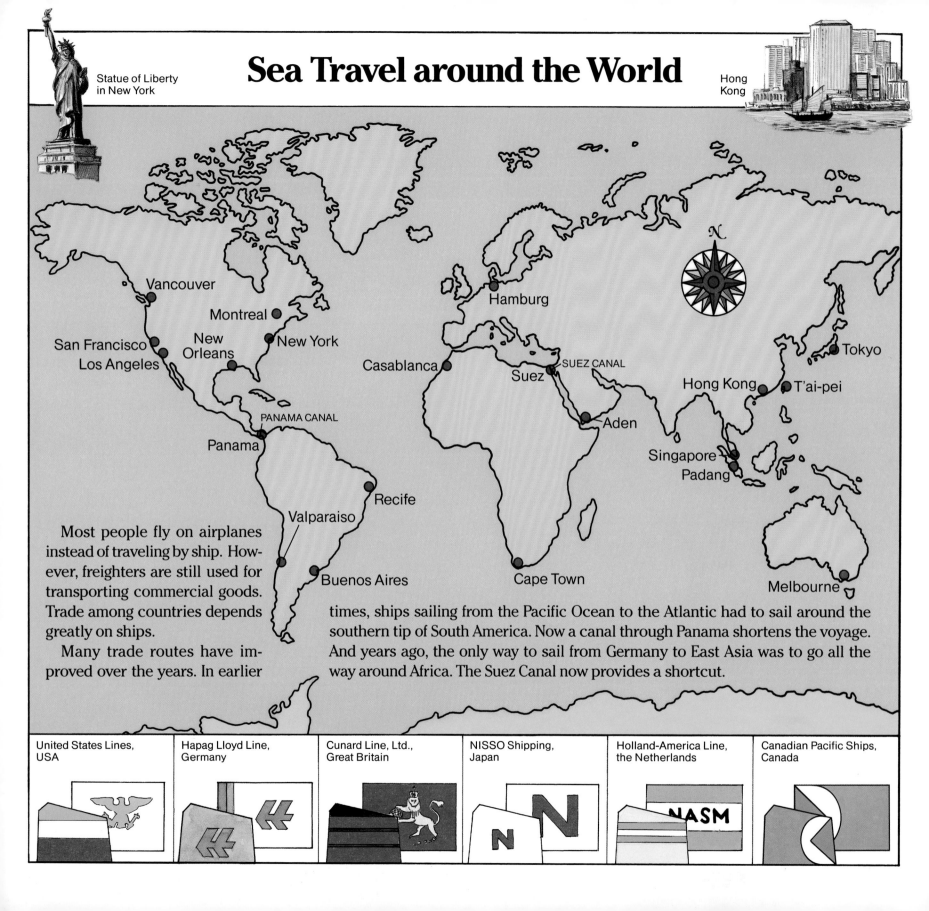

Sea Travel around the World

Statue of Liberty in New York

Hong Kong

Vancouver
Montreal
San Francisco
New Orleans
Los Angeles
New York
Panama
PANAMA CANAL
Recife
Valparaiso
Buenos Aires

Hamburg
Casablanca
Suez   SUEZ CANAL
Aden
Cape Town

Hong Kong
Tokyo
T'ai-pei
Singapore
Padang
Melbourne

Most people fly on airplanes instead of traveling by ship. However, freighters are still used for transporting commercial goods. Trade among countries depends greatly on ships.

Many trade routes have improved over the years. In earlier times, ships sailing from the Pacific Ocean to the Atlantic had to sail around the southern tip of South America. Now a canal through Panama shortens the voyage. And years ago, the only way to sail from Germany to East Asia was to go all the way around Africa. The Suez Canal now provides a shortcut.

| United States Lines, USA | Hapag Lloyd Line, Germany | Cunard Line, Ltd., Great Britain | NISSO Shipping, Japan | Holland-America Line, the Netherlands | Canadian Pacific Ships, Canada |

ABC of Sea Travel

abaft: toward the stern

aft: at or near the ship's stern

aftership: the rear part of a ship

amidships: in the middle of a ship

anchor: a heavy piece of iron, which digs into the sea floor to hold a ship to a spot

astern: behind the stern

beam: the width of a ship

belay: a command to stop

berth: a place where a ship ties up or lays anchor

boatswain: (pronounced BO-sun) the ship's officer in charge of all work done on deck

bow: the front of a ship

bowsprit: a pole projecting from the bow, to which sails are attached

bridge: the command post on ship for steering

broadside: cannons positioned to fire through portholes cut in the side of a ship

bulkhead: a watertight partition in the ship's hull

buoy: a floating signal anchored to the sea floor

buoyancy: 1. the capacity of water to hold an object up 2. the capacity to float

cabin: officers' quarters

capsize: to tip over; to overturn

captain: the commander of a ship

compass: a device used for determining directions

deck: a ship's floor

derrick: a crane used for unloading cargo from a ship's hold

dock: the area of a harbor where ships are loaded and unloaded

fathom: a unit of measure, used for measuring the depth of water. One fathom equals six feet.

fore: toward the front (bow) of a ship

forecastle: (pronounced FOLK-sull) the raised deck at the bow

foremast: the frontmost mast of a ship

funnel: a ship's chimney or smokestack

galley: 1. a ship's kitchen 2. a long, narrow boat powered by a row of paddles

gangway: a footbridge to the ship

hatch: an opening or door in the deck or side

heave: to set off; to weigh anchor

helm: the steering control of a ship

hold: a cargo area below deck

hull: the body of a ship

jack ladder: steps that hang overboard

keel: the backbone of a ship

knots: a ship's speed in nautical miles per hour (a nautical mile equals 6,080 feet per hour)

lateen: a type of triangular sail

lee: the side of the ship that faces away from the wind

load lines: lines painted on the side of a ship to show how full a ship may be loaded

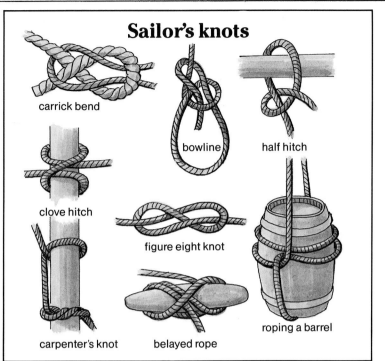

Sailor's knots

carrick bend

bowline

half hitch

clove hitch

figure eight knot

carpenter's knot

belayed rope

roping a barrel

mainmast: the tallest and strongest mast, in the middle of a ship

mayday: a distress signal meaning "help me"

mess: a ship's dining room

mizzenmast: the rearmost mast of a ship

moor: to secure a ship, by dropping anchor or by tying it to a mooring post

mooring post: a post for securing a ship's ropes

orlop: the lowest deck of a sailing ship

pilot: the nautical consultant to the captain

poop: a raised deck at the stern of the ship

port: the left side of a ship

porthole: a round window

propeller: a device with turning blades that propels, or moves, a ship

prow: the front of a ship; bow

reef: to shorten a ships' sails

rigging: the sails with their masts and ropes

rudder: a flat blade of wood or metal at the stern, which is turned to steer a ship

sextant: a navigation instrument used to determine a ship's position

skipper: the captain of a small ship

starboard: the right side of a ship

stern: the rear part of a ship

wreck: a ship that can no longer be used, because of age or because of damage

Author Siegfried Aust loves both technology and writing for children. Aust has combined his interests in the Fun with Technology series. He is a teacher who has written many books for young readers.

Illustrator Enno Kleinert lives in Munich, Germany. He paints many subjects, but his great love is painting ships and nautical scenes. Kleinert's nautical paintings have been featured in many exhibits.

This edition first published 1993 by Lerner Publications Company. All English language rights reserved.

Original edition copyright © 1990 by Verlag Carl Ueberreuter, Vienna, under the title KOMM MIT AN BORD. Translation copyright © 1993 by Lerner Publications Company.

Translated from the German by Amy Gelman.

Library of Congress Cataloging-in-Publication Data

Aust, Siegfried.
 [Komm mit an bord. English]
 Ships! : come aboard / Siegfried Aust ; illustrated by Enno Kleinert.
  p. cm.
 Translation of: Komm mit an bord.
 Summary: Traces the history of water transportation from rafts and kayaks to modern ocean liners and war ships. Includes related activities.
 ISBN 0-8225-2156-3
 1. Ships—History—Juvenile literature. [1. Ships—History.]
I. Kleinert, Enno, ill. II. Title.
VM150.A8713 1992
387.2′09—dc20   92-12761
                                                    CIP
                                                    AC

Manufactured in the United States of America

1 2 3 4 5 6 98 97 96 95 94 93